In the Colonie

A Memoir of Separation and Belonging

MICHAEL ROSEN

PENGUIN BOOKS

PENGUIN BOOKS

Published by the Penguin Group
Penguin Books Ltd, 80 Strand, London WC2R ORL, England
Penguin Group (USA) Inc., 375 Hudson Street, New York, New York 10014, USA
Penguin Books Australia Ltd, 250 Camberwell Road, Camberwell, Victoria 3124, Australia
Penguin Books Canada Ltd, 10 Alcorn Avenue, Toronto, Ontario, Canada M4V 3B2
Penguin Books India (P) Ltd, 11 Community Centre, Panchsheel Park, New Delhi – 110 017, India
Penguin Group (NZ), cnr Airborne and Rosedale Roads, Albany, Auckland 1310, New Zealand
Penguin Books (South Africa) (Pty) Ltd, 24 Sturdee Avenue, Rosebank 2196, South Africa

Penguin Books Ltd, Registered Offices: 80 Strand, London WC2R ORL, England

www.penguin.com

Published in Penguin Books 2005
1

The moral right of the author has been asserted

Set in 10.5/14.75 pt Minion
Typeset by Rowland Phototypesetting Ltd, Bury St Edmunds, Suffolk
Printed in England by Clays Ltd, St Ives plc

dear e. love mx

'Do you want an explanation?' the Traveller asked. The officer nodded in silence. 'I'm opposed to this procedure,' the Traveller now said . . .'

from *In the Penal Colony* by Franz Kafka

My mother told me that at the end of my first week at Nursery School, when I was three, she went in to have a chat with the teacher. How's things going with him? my mother asked. Everything's fine, said the teacher, but do you want to leave him out of religious things? Why's that? said my mother. Well, said the teacher, before we eat, we all stand up, put our hands together and close our eyes and we say, 'Thank you, God, for the food we eat,' but Michael won't stand up. He stays sitting in his chair, shouting: No thank you God, no thank you God.

It was their front rooms. No one was ever in their front rooms. The curtains in the windows were open but it was always dark behind. The houses looked out on to the streets with their eyes shut. I knew there were people inside, but they stayed in the back. Sometimes I met them: they were my friends' parents and they told us not to go into the front room. I asked my friends why not and all they could say was that it was what they were told. I understood that their parents thought other people shouldn't see you as you sat down to listen to the wireless.

We roamed round the streets together but when we got to the end of his road he said that I couldn't come any further. He said that he wasn't allowed to play with me and he didn't want his parents to see that he'd been with me. So I'd stop by the United Services Club on the corner. By peering round the end of the hedge I could watch him walk up the road to his house.

Watching television cowboys was how they learned to gallop; peeoo peeoo (that was the gun) and they smacked their bums (the horse's back). We had the wireless: And now for our serial: 'The Eagle of the Ninth.' It was the end of the Empire. Hundreds of Roman soldiers had headed north and disappeared. I ran home to go looking for them. At school we mapped the Queen's visit to Australia all along the classroom wall. Can you bring in pictures? No, there aren't any pictures of the Queen in the *Daily Worker*. And soldiers, please. She wanted soldiers; there was trouble in Kenya but there was good news: locking them up seemed to be working, she said. Hopalong Cassidy, Cisco Kid, peeoo peeoo, who are you?

I found my way into the Catholic Church
fête and walked about on my own. I knew that I
wasn't Catholic. There was a plate-breaking
competition. People queued up to throw things at
plates. And there was a tent. Inside, there was a
puppet show. A row of onions bobbed up and
down. In the middle of the onions a flower waved
about. A gramophone record was playing a song:
'I'm a lonely little petunia in an onion patch.' The
flower waved about in time to the music. Then
the song went 'boo hoo boo hoo' and all the onions
bobbed up and down in time. An hour or so later,
back at home, my mother asked me where I had
been. I said that I had gone to the Catholic Church
fête. On your own? she said. Yes, I said. Later, at
bedtime, I asked her if she knew a song about a
petunia and some onions. Yes, she said. How does
it go? I said. She said: I'm a lonely little petunia
in an onion patch, an onion patch, an onion patch
why do you ask? They were singing it at the
Catholic Church fête. Who were? The puppets.
Did you see anybody you knew? she said. No, I said.

In the rough grass in the Memorial Park, where the mowers didn't mow, there were two drain covers. Someone said that they were bomb shelters and we made plans. One of us nicked a crowbar out of a dad's toolbox and we levered them open. There was a ladder and we climbed down into the room below. There was broken china and glass; earth on the floor. To one side were beds with blankets. Someone said that we could make it our den; I said that it was like when they opened up the pyramids and grave robbers had got there first but it was thousands of years before. And it really was ages ago, said someone, the war ended ten years ago, you know. Soldiers must have died down here, you know. We looked at the blankets where the soldiers must have died. Then someone said, what if we were all down here and it was our den and one of Sherbet-jacket's gang came by and shut the lid?

Os gerissen zolste weren, says my father
Don't say those things, says my mother
'ch 'a' dich im loch, he says
Don't say those things, she says
What's he to Hecuba? he says
The coat's nice. Wear it. They're wearing them like that, she says
No job takes two minutes, he says
So? Did they like the coat? she says
Never believe a rumour till it's officially denied, he says
Leave him alone, he's tired, she says
Ah, the whirligig of time, he says
It's not burnt. It's crisp, she says
Your muscles stand out like sparrow's kneecaps, he says
Stalin must have been ga-ga, she says
Genug is' genug, he says
What's the use of a frying pan without a handle? she says
You look as sharp as a *matzo* ball and twice as greasy, he says
Don't pick it, wash it, she says
My *zeyde* used to say: One match, you can break. Two matches,
you can break. A whole box of matches, you can't break. That's a
union, he says
My greatest horror was bedbugs, she says
Why don't you have some bread with your jam? he says
Seeing the dray horses slipping on the ice used to terrify me,

7

she says
What do you think this is, Liberty Hall? he says
No one else was defending us against the fascists,
so of course we joined, she says
Tout va bien, Madam' de la Marquise, he says
The lettuce needs cheering up, she says
What larks, Pip, he says
It's the way you're sitting, she says
Herrel shmerel went to the races,
lost his *gatkes* and his braces, he says
You knew which ones were the doodlebugs, she says
So they call you *pisher*! he says

A girl in the park asked me what shows I had seen for my Christmas treat. I said that it was called *The Big Rock Candy Mountain*. Was it on ice? she said. No, it was in a theatre, I said. I love shows in the theatre, she said, my mother took me to see *The Pyjama Game*, it was ever so saucy, she said. Their pyjamas only came down to here, you could see everything. What was your show like? I said that a man called Alan Lomax stood at the side of the stage and he was meant to be some kind of tramp and it was a trip across America and they sang songs. Oh, she said, yes, I love musicals, when we went to see *Aladdin on Ice* that was like a musical. What sort of songs did they sing at yours? she said. I said that they kept singing 'The Big Rock Candy Mountain, where the bulldogs all have rubber teeth and something about the buzzing of the bees in the cigarette trees and a soda water fountain'. That sounds nice, she said, and did they dance? They danced in my show, she said. Yes, I said, there was one thing where the men were building the railway and they sang, 'Take this hammer, Whoa! Carry it to the captain, whoa!' Were there any saucy bits? she asked. And I said, No, I didn't think so, and she was disappointed for me.

My father once tried to explain to me what
was wrong with their houses: mock-Tudor,
he said, phoney baroney – look at it. Each
one trying to look like something that it isn't.
If there was somewhere else better, more real,
more true to itself, he never told us where it
was. All the while he carried out guerrilla
attacks. He started with a builder's dump
which lay heaped up in a yard out the back of
our flat. Every Sunday, he raided it
for old sinks, lengths of tubing, plugs,
lampshades, taps – stuff that had been ripped
out of the houses he hated. If he saw something
out of reach, he would send me clambering up
the pile to pull out a lavatory chain or a
ballcock. It seemed to make him happy claiming
this stuff. But what made him really joyful was
when we went raiding empty houses. He
seemed to know where and when people
moved out. Around the fringes of where we
lived there were big, old houses, often set in
long, wide gardens; places that had become
run down and the people had gone or died.
We would head out on a Sunday morning to

find them. Sometimes he'd send me in to see if there was anything inside. Sometimes he'd come in too and we'd scurry about, looking for things. I remember old armchairs, mirrors, wardrobes, brown carpets. Places where you could look out of the windows and see a lawn and hedges. We took a torch and one time I went up into the loft. Something caught his eye. It didn't look much. He sent me crawling across to fetch it. It was some kind of jug or vase. He wiped the coat of dust off it and you could see a dark-green glaze. It was a big pot with two handles, rippled, as if it had been made out of coils. Grab that, he said.

My best friend knew the names for different kinds of apples, different kinds of birds, different kinds of cars, how to grow potatoes, how to paint a wall, how to make cement, how to get to Gillingham, how to make a go-kart, the whole of 'My nose is cold, tiddly pom' and scores of rhymes about bums and farting. We lived in each other's houses, climbed into the builder's store and made a den. We spotted a bullfinch in the woods next to the bypass and caught newts in the scraggy pond there. He wrote to me from Gillingham and Brixham, I wrote to him from Skenfrith and the Jura Mountains. He failed his eleven-plus. I passed it. He slowly stopped being my best friend. For years I wrote about him, us and the go-kart, us and gymnastics on the sofa, us and Baldy, us and the tunnel, us and Old Man Adams. There was more to write: us and the tree house we never finished, the firework night where the whole lot blew up. One day, I thought, I'll bump into him and tell him how I've been acting out him and me and the go-kart for years in front of kids in schools. It's been my way of saying sorry that I had turned the thing over with him on the back. When I was forty I found out that he died when he was seventeen.

My brother and I were put on a train out of Weimar and we headed off into the Thuringianwald, a forest somewhere near Czechoslovakia, I was told. My brother was to stay in one house and I would stay in another. It's all right, they said, there's someone in the family who speaks English. My family seemed to be some kind of farmers. Well, they had chickens in their garden and I was put to play with two children, a boy and a girl, who were a bit younger than me and who kept saying: 'Kick me,' and running away. The one who spoke English was a big girl who I thought was as beautiful as a film star, tall, with long blonde hair and a skin so white that it was almost grey. She seemed downcast or lost. Surely my big brother would go crazy about her, but he seemed more interested in the one in his house who opened her mouth and laughed. I went to bed in an alcove, in a bed that had a high wooden side. One night the big blonde girl came and sat by my bed and asked me about my brother and then sat next to me saying nothing, looking at me as I had looked at a bird

14

that once flew into our front room at home,
something that belonged elsewhere now up closer
than ever before. She said that she hoped that
I was happy. I said I was. I didn't know why
she stared at me in my wooden bed in the
alcove and I didn't say that I had no idea where
I was or who she and her family were. One day
we climbed to the top of a mountain that they
were proud of and my brother walked along the
forest path ahead of me, strolling between the
beautiful girls, talking in German while the
children with me ran about under the pine trees,
calling out, 'Kick me, kick me.' Afterwards my
brother explained to me that he wouldn't be able
to see them again. Not ever. He wouldn't be
allowed to come and they wouldn't be allowed
out of East Germany.

Good things were a long way off. It always needed
a bus and a train. Like for those New Years' do's
where I was allowed to stay up and listen to
Malcolm the actor and Solly the Communist
councillor's jokes. What was so funny about
Hymie getting lost in the Alps and when the Red
Cross man came, him saying, 'I've given already?'
It was a bus, a train and another bus to the place
behind the cinema where they were building a theatre.
All they had was an old tin chapel and a new hall
they called the Stanislavsky Room. In the chapel
I sat on my own, watching a play about a landlady
and a man tearing paper. Then someone went crazy
and grabbed him. A Jewish bloke got nasty. On
Friday nights we would practise Stanislavsky in the
Stanislavsky Room: mime peeling an apple, to show
us how it isn't a potato. I had to grab a girl's hand
and say that I loved her more than the moon. It was
down to me to say that, because there weren't any
other boys. It wasn't supposed to matter that I was
twelve and they were fifteen and sixteen and
seventeen and tried to be kind to me. Your eyes are
like the stars, marry me, marry me in the Stanislavsky
Room. Then out past the tin chapel, back on the bus,

back on the train, back on the bus, the houses' eyes shut.

When the kids and the *moniteurs* of the *colonie* in Normandy asked us to sing a song, the only one that we could manage was 'My bonny lies over the ocean'. The three of us stood in a row in the tent while everyone else sat at their tables watching: 'Bring back, bring back, bring back my bonny to me'. So when we went on a visit to Omaha Beach where the Americans landed on D-Day, some of them sang 'ma bonni la ise au verre ze auchanne'. I slept in the bed next to Jacques; he lent me his comic books and showed me how to fold my sheet over. We swapped addresses. Two boys talked to me in the tent after he'd gone out and said that I shouldn't be his friend. He's *indochine*, Indo-Chinese. I heard it as: *un dos chine*, a Chinese back? What's the matter with that? I thought. He's a liar, they said, *menteur*. I tried to stay in with everyone but Jacques noticed that I wasn't standing next to him as we all stood in the road to watch the Tour de France come by. He asked me if the others had said anything about him. I said I didn't know, but I could see that he knew they had. And I didn't know then what General Giap had done, but perhaps Jacques did.

Back in England, in Northumberland I left the family by the campfire and went up on the moor on my own with Grant the farmer. He showed me a sheep that had got stuck in a hollow in the heather, the wool had taken up rain and it couldn't get up. It was dying. We gripped its legs, buried our hands in its wet fleece and heaved till it could get going on its own. In the stable he had a cow with milk fever. He punched a needle into its haunch; its eyes showed white and started to roll. You're afraid she'll die, aren't you? I'm not afraid of death, he said, you are. Your parents are atheists, aren't they? Could you kill a man? I had to choose: kill or be killed, he said. I went back to the family by the fire and told them about the sheep and the cow but I didn't tell them what Grant had said.

I came back from school, full of Dave's holiday news about kibbutzim. It's socialism, I said. Who for? said my father. For the people, I said. Dave says they share everything. Which people is this? said my father, can anyone live there? No, I don't think so, this is for Jews, I said. Oh, I see, he said, socialism for one people? Yes, I said. Isn't that called National Socialism? he said. But that led to terrible things, I said. That's true, he said.

I ran away from home. I said, I'm going on the Aldermaston March to ban the bomb. They said that this was out of the question, the boy's mad. Crazy. My mother said, Where will you stay? You'd have nothing to eat, you don't know anyone, what would you eat? You're not going. Harold, say something, he's too young, look at him, he's packing. You can't go without a spare pair of trousers, how can he carry a bag like that for twenty miles a day? Stop him, Harold. What would you do in the evening? You need to eat, you get ill if you don't eat. Take a tin of beans. You can always eat beans. Harold, stop him. There's the chicken. Take the chicken. If you're taking a tin of beans, take two. He's thirteen, Harold. Go next year, wait till next year, they won't have banned the bomb by then, believe me. There'll be another march. Go on that one. You must keep eating fresh fruit. And you like dates. He's always liked dates, hasn't he, Harold? Just squeeze them in down the side of the bag. Couldn't he wait till the last day, when we'll be there? We can all go to Trafalgar Square together. Harold, have you got the chicken?

Just because it's Easter, doesn't mean it's warm.
It can snow at Easter. Wear the string vest. Who's
organized the coaches? Do we know these people,
Harold? One orange! Take five. And raisins. He's
thirteen. It's ridiculous. He can't go. Keep the
chicken wrapped. Phone us if you need more food.
Goodbye.

Inside the marquee there were thousands of us
and the papers said that we were all doing sex and
wearing duffle coats. There was the Rapacki Plan.
A neutral Europe. That sounded good. Science for
Peace. That sounded good, but someone said that it
was run by the Communists and they shouldn't be
there because they thought the Russian bomb was
OK. I'm not a Communist any more, I said. The
government think they can win a nuclear war, said
someone. They've built Regional Seats of Government
for themselves. Underground. We should nationalize
the arms industry, said someone. Over there's the girl
I married in the Stanislavsky Room. Sweden hasn't got
nuclear weapons. We should all go off to one of the
RSGs and sit on it. Gandhi. Peaceful disobedience.
Over there's my brother's friend Jeff who's got the
Blind Lemon Jefferson record. Gonna lay down my
sword and shield, echo like the crack of doom, I belong
to a family the biggest on earth, tea round the corner,
close up the gaps, keep it coming Billericay, this is
nothing like school, nothing like school, nothing like
school, he's an anarchist, are you an anarchist? Hey
baby, the monster's in the loch, so what are we, then,
Left Labour? Labour Left? New Left? we got the desert

boots, what else do we need, strangers are friends, I think you are the most beautifully exciting oh shit not that I'm saying that, I just look at her a lot when the saints come marching in, over there's Humph

We had been driving too long, me in the back discovering only-childness, what with my brother off somewhere in the mountains with a tent. We stopped by a bend in the river where a rock and a beach offered a place to swim. Hot, late afternoon. There was a girl in the water and she figured I was English. Her grandmother urged her to give it a go. I said she didn't need to, I spoke French. But her grandmother said she should. We swam to the other side, and we sat on stones. It was the first time I had seen a black swimming costume that had no back. She sat in a place where she had to look over her shoulder at me. She said she wanted someone to write to in England. We swam back and she made her grandmother take my address. I took hers. In the car, my mother said to my father, 'We didn't have to go so soon, did we? We could have stayed longer. You could see that he wanted to stay.' She turned to me. 'Tell him you wanted to

stay.' A few months later I got a card
that said, *Le soleil, l'eau, un soir, un
rêve*, the sun, the water, an evening,
a dream. That's all. I couldn't write back.
I'd lost her address. She never wrote again.

I came back saying that everyone was moaning about the buses being stopped because of the dispute. My mother said, Then I'd better give you some money to put in their strike-fund bucket at the garage.

I am now doing what my parents did with me: bringing up a child just a few years after a son had died. I didn't know that I was one-who-came-after until I was ten. Going through photos and asking who was that baby on my mother's knee. My father saying it was the baby who died. My mother never mentioning it, never saying it, no conversation with her about it ever. It took our child coming along, fifty-four years after I was born for me to realize that my parents were people who thought about how they had lost a child. It had never crossed my mind before then. So, from the age of ten, I knew that there had been a brother before me, and yet I never looked at my mother or father and thought that the things they said or did might have been that way because of what had happened to their baby. When I was sixteen I went away to France for six weeks. My father was going to take me to the station, my mother was leaving for work. She was going to leave the house before me. I said goodbye to her. She

didn't go. She went upstairs to fetch something
and came down again. My father waved his
hand at me. 'What?' I said. 'Your mother. Go
to her. She's upset.' 'I've been away before,
haven't I?' I said, but really I was thinking
of my brother. He had been away this long
several times and there hadn't been any big
scene when he went. But now, from where
I'm standing today, I can see that he was
different. He was older than the one who
died. He came before. I came after. I went
to her but she said not to fuss, and she went
off to work. Not to fuss. And now this little
one. Look what she did today. She put her
hand in the plant pot, filled her hand with
gravel and threw it on the kitchen floor.
Don't do that, you said, and she did it again.
And again. So I took her up the garden
and she said, 'I throw stonies.' And laughed.
What happens now? Do we try to make sure
she knows that we don't want this to happen?
I'm about to go to the Turkish supermarket to
buy some hummus. Do we go through some
routine where we say that she can come if

she stops throwing stones or will it all seem
like life's too short, yes, just that, too bloody
short. Well, my love, you shut the back door,
how unlike you, while we stayed out in the
garden, and our little one was unhappy
because she wanted to come in and I said
that you were cross, there were all the stones
to clear up. And she said sorry and we did go
to the Turkish supermarket and we bought
hummus and when we got back, my love,
you and me, we sat outside in the evening sun
and drank cold Turkish beer. *Efes*. How he
loved *Efes*. How we're loving this *Efes*.

I thought it was the journey there that was worrying
her. I was the only sixteen-year-old she'd heard
of who would have to get themselves from London
to the Ardèche by themselves. I was the only one
I knew too. My father thought he'd make it safe
(for me? for him?) by running through the details:
Dover, Calais, Gare du Nord, *métro* to Gare de
Lyon, Valence, Aubenas and there you'll be met
by Mme Goetschy. There, that easy. Like holding
your breath till you get there. Like holding my
breath in the *gourde*, the pool in the river where
I'd met them all last year. Would the same ones
be there again this year? Benzizi the brown-
skinned midget? Goddemarre the Elvis? Maurice
the communist *moniteur*? Alice the Moroccan?
Mercedez the Spanish nun (not really, she was
fifteen but looked like that)? And the heat. It
would be hot like that again, wouldn't it? French
money, English money, travellers' cheques. All
to go in the maroon Moroccan-leather wallet.
– What's he going to wear, Harold?
– He's got his anorak.
– It's too small. It doesn't fit. He can't wear that.
– All right. He can have mine.
His? The East German anorak? Bought five years

earlier in Weimar. Or was in it East Berlin, where I'd
discovered *Bratwurst mit Senf?* I'd always loved
that anorak, with its soft tartan lining. Faded blue.
I loved that faded blue.
– And you can put the wallet in the front pocket.
  Then you'll know where it is.
Like Kästner's Emil Tischbein off on the train to
Berlin, but my money not like his pinned to the
inside of his pocket where the thief got it. Mine,
in the wallet, in the German Communist anorak.
Paris was hot. The Gare de Lyon was hot. Look
at me. Sitting in a café in Paris on my own.
Drinking *jus de pommes.* Out of all the people
from school I'm the only person I know who's
ever drunk *jus de pommes.* And I've gone in there
and said, *un jus de pommes s'il vous plaît* and here
I am drinking it. At three minutes before midnight,
the train groaned out. I stood looking out at the waves
of apartments and I thought of the thousands and
hundreds of thousands and millions of *petits pois et
lardons* sitting in the cupboards of the buildings. I
thought of how school had ended with a coach trip
and sad snogging and I realized I had left the anorak
hanging from a door handle in the café.

I once arranged for a German boy to come and stay so that my boy could speak some German for his GCSE. He was a bewildered creature who blurted out facts about America and reasons why boys shouldn't clear up. He wanted to play with baby toys. When I told him (because he asked me about why I had a German name) that I was Jewish he said that that wasn't possible. I asked him about his name. His parents were Hungarian, he said. I said I didn't think that that was impossible. When he was leaving, we sat in the departure lounge at Heathrow; we didn't look at each other. I saw a man, an actor, who wrote a book about being a father, or divorce, or both, and he was there with his son, the one he had written about, and he was arguing with him about what was in his bag or what wasn't in his bag and then he said goodbye and tried to hug the boy. But the boy was ratty and just turned away. Then I said goodbye to the German boy and it was so cold and he was so far off and looked so keen to get away from me. I felt bad that I had got it wrong and I remembered Mme Goetschy meeting me on Aubenas station. Tiny Mme Goetschy, never out of her black swimsuit, always tucking in the edges of her bum, her side-teeth silvered, always on show with her laughing and laughing.

– It's going to be a good *colonie* this year, she said and reached up to hug me and kiss me and hug me again.

– *Comme t'es grand*, Mike. You're so big. One metre eighty? Everyone's here. This year you can't drive to the place. Or walk there. You have to go over the river. You have to pull on the wires.

She took her hands off the steering wheel and pulled on imaginary wires. I slid about on the metal floor in the back of her 2-cv van, bouncing up into the mountains.

– Oh it's marvellous you've come. You remember, Alain? Maurice?

I said I did but there were always people called Alain and Maurice. Next to her on the front seat was Jules. Dark Jules, dark skin, black hair, long stiff neck. Wasn't he the kid no one liked and there was a fight last year when someone said that his bed smelt of wee? At least that's what I thought they said. *Pisse-en-lit*. It does mean dandelion, though.

The year before, my father had said that as
I had got on with them all so well, swimming
at the *gourde*, would I like to stop goofing around
with him and Mum and stay with these *colonie*
kids for the last five days of the holiday? He just
went up to the *moniteur* and said, How about it?
And a few days later I was in a tent making
lavender bottles with them all: bending lavender
flowers down into the stalks and weaving ribbon
in and out till they were tight, like, as they said,
bottles. The Ardèche was hot and dry like a desert.
The thyme went brown; there was lavender under
our fingernails.
– Make more lavender bottles? Who does he
   think we are, slaves?
That was Benzizi. No one spoke English. I had to
become French all day. And we did *Don Quichotte*.
Maurice, the communist *moniteur*, shouted at them
to learn their lines, make props. Sun-burned Etienne
wearing a colander and wielding a broom was Don
Quixote, little Benzizi was Sancho Pancha with my
striped towel over his shoulder. Mercedez was the
beautiful woman. Alice was the narrator. There
wasn't time to put me in the play, Maurice said.

On the day before the show, he stopped everything and said that he was disgusted by them all. They were a generation of don't-carers. None of them thought about the future, only the present. All their ideas came from bad films and bad music.

– Your parents are all workers and trade unionists. They work their hearts out day after day in the Gerland Chemical Factory; they support the union and it's the union that's sorted it out for all of you to come to a place like this so that you don't spend the whole summer hanging around with yobs. But you say you don't care. I'm depressed, he said. I worry about what's going to happen to you, I worry about what's going to happen to France.

In the tent afterwards, Benzizi said that he was going to organize a strike. Was I with them or against them? I thought, how can you organize a strike against a Communist? I looked up the word for a guest. It said it was the same word for a host. I said, I am a guest (or host) and I didn't know if I could go on strike.

– *Merde*, said Etienne.

So I said that I wasn't against the strike.

– *Moi, je suis communiste*, said Benzizi

– *Moi aussi*, I said, me too.

Mme Goetschy came down and sat on the floor
and said that it was sad, sad, sad. Soon everyone
would be back in Lyon, back at school, the
colonie would be finished. Let's not have a sad
end. Maurice cares about you. He wants you to
have everything in life. Not to be satisfied with
what you've been given.

– We're not slaves, said Benzizi.

– I agree, said Mme Goetschy.

We played *Don Quichotte*, lit by a bulkhead
light off the side of the shower-block. Don Quixote
and Sancho Panza tilted at cardboard boxes; the
little ones giggled and screamed. My dad had tears
in his eyes. Perfect, perfect, he said, pure Brecht,
pure Brecht. That Maurice, what a man, what a
man.

Pull on the wires. This year we would reach the
colonie on a chariot. Everything and everybody
would get to the tents, the shower- and the cooking-
blocks on a chariot over the river. There was no
other way. The 2-cv could go no further. You stand
on the platform and pull one wire, while over your
head the chariot's wheels ran round, locked under
the other wire.

– *Vas-y*, Mike, Dark Jules said, off you go, and
  Mme Goetschy laughed till the silver showed.
– *Maman, maman!* – (There was a baby on the
  other side of the river.)
– See! It's Mike, she called back to the baby.
– You've had a baby? I said. That was quick.
– Normal, she said. No faster than usual.

So I climbed up. Mme Goetschy and Jules watched
from one side; the baby and Mme Goetschy's sister
from the other. In the middle it lurched and invited
me into the water. And I'm smelling all over of
London – though this year I've got flip-flops and
boxers. What's the big deal with these rubber
slipper things you keep going on about? What's the
matter with your sandals? my father had said. Yes,
said my mother, sandals are good. Everyone wears

38

sandals. They don't, I said. No one wears bloody sandals. I've got to have flip-flops. I must have them. This year I couldn't have the kids asking me again why I wore strange things.

I got to love the way the chariot was lurching. We would get up there in twos and threes, me, tiny Benzizi, Maurice the footballer, Pink Nicolas, and sit on the hot wood and dive or fall or bomb off it, feel the rush of the water, over and over. We would sit with our legs dangling, looking between our knees; we would nudge and shove till we flailed about in the air and smacked the river. It was something we had to go on and on doing. You could pull the chariot fast and fall off the back. You could hang like a cowboy on a cliff edge. You could take off screaming or roll off dead. You could sit in the heat, pulling your sunburn off and dropping it into the water, and talk about the girls one by one, every single one of them. It was a place to be that was so far and so long away.

I rehearsed a phone call home. All that money. And the anorak. I rang and I told them about how the journey was fine, and Mme Goetschy was there to meet me, and this year we were in a place by the river, we're in a horseshoe, we're surrounded by cliffs, it looks like Lone Ranger country; you can only get to it by a chariot over the river and I left the anorak at the Gare de Lyon with all the money in it. It was my father, and I could hear a look. It was the one he did when he looked across the room to my mother. And I could hear her look back. And the lips. If things weren't going well, they were both very good at lip work. It was soundless tutting.

– You're not to worry, he said. If it's lost, it's lost and we'll claim it off the insurance. You make sure you have a good time. And write. Tell us how it is.

Mme Goetschy said that she rang the Gare de Lyon, but nothing.

Benzizi was older and louder than me but he had
stopped growing sometime when he was about ten.
His skin was so brown that if he got in a fight, the
scratch marks were white. The only people I had
ever seen who looked like him were Brazilian
footballers. He had learnt to collect guardians:
Maurice the footballer, who also looked Brazilian,
and Goddemarre the Elvis who had two sayings:
Qu'est-ce que c'est ce bouleau? Which I sensed
meant something like, what's the point of this work?
And, *Ça va, la foule?* How you doing, you lot?
Maurice did keepy-uppies while he sang: *Allez l'O. L.,
allez l'O. L., allez*; Goddemarre combed his hair and
straightened his jeans down his legs and word went
round that he was seriously bad back home in Lyon.
He'd done things. No one would say what. Benzizi
was in love with Françoise, he said. He said she was
the most beautiful woman (woman?) he had ever
known. I thought so too, but I said nothing. But then,
I had thought Alice and Mercedez were; they weren't
here this year. And this year the girls wore a bikini
that was like a swimsuit that had the middle cut out of
it. All of them, apart from Nicole, who wore what
looked like three tiny blue hankies. They poured

Nivea on their arms and it was beyond belief to think that as they sat on the stones by the river, their nakednesses were only seconds away. I had never been so close for so long to so many girls wearing so little and they all seemed so completely, so totally, so calmly uninterested in any of us. They seemed to love each other, smoothing in the Nivea, washing and brushing each other's hair, painting each other's nails, moving each other's bikinis and T-shirts into the right place, swapping jeans, telling each other what they looked like from behind, going off to the shower room, locking the door and laughing in there for hours.

This year our *moniteur* was Henri, who said he didn't believe; he had his beliefs but it was a long story. For the whole six weeks he wore the same pair of leopard-skin nylon boxers. He looked like a Brazilian footballer too. As he lay on the bed next to mine in our tent at siesta time, I looked at his hair. It was frizzy and crinkly, like a black lamb's. Alain the trainee electrician rigged up a record player outside between the fig trees, Benzizi played Les Platters, four black men who sang 'Sixteen Tons', and Ray Charles, who sang 'Georgia, Georgia' and 'Let me hear you say, yeah'. Benzizi could do a Ray Charles 'Yeah-eah-eah' perfectly and he said that I ought to be able to too but he left me alone while he jived with Françoise, who stood a foot taller than him. Henri interrupted Ray Charles with a jazz cabaret big-band singer called Léo Ferré who sang about a beautiful girl who he called *Jolie Môme*, beautiful Paris which he called *Paname*, and a hard-labour camp on the Ile de Ré where the men sang, 'Merde à Vauban' – shit to Vauban, who Henri explained was a famous nineteenth-century civil engineer. Benzizi rocked his head back, hung out his little hands in an Elvis way and sang, 'Yeah-eah-eah.'

They kept saying: *je m'en fous*. I didn't
know what it meant. They said it meant,
ce fait rien, *je m'en fiche*, it doesn't matter,
I don't care. I tried to imagine it on the
page: 'je menfous', perhaps. Is it then 'tu
menfous, il menfout'? I said, how does it
conjugate? I was asking Benzizi and
Goddemarre who, I hadn't clocked, weren't
that bothered with school and, like their
fathers, would soon be working in the
Gerland Chemical Factory. They were
helpless, slapping each other, laughing.
They were trying to explain that it meant
'I don't give a fuck', or literally, 'I fuck myself
about it', so it had to be *tu t'en fous* . . . you fuck
yourself about it, not: 'tu m'en fous', which
would mean you fuck *me* about it. They cried
and laughed, stopped and then cried all over
again.

Our tent stood on an old vine terrace where vines still grew, and Maurice the footballer raided them, grabbing the bunches, holding them above his mouth and running his lips over the grapes as a camel would, pulling them into his mouth. He laughed at me trying eat them one by one, spitting the pips out.

– Just scoff them, *bouffe*, *bouffe*, he shouted.
Our tent smelt of armpits, grit, hot canvas and old comic books. Nothing covered the ground apart from old duckboards, *caillebottis*, so our beds worked their way into the earth. When we lay on our backs on our beds in the afternoons, we'd watch the sweat swell out of our chests, the beasts run over the roof: the plastic-bucket-green praying mantis stalking the flying grasshopper with a spike sticking out of her rear, horseflies as big as your thumb planning their next plunge into your arm, and ants climbing the legs of the beds. What were they all for, these things? Someone left a cigarette end in the rubbish basket while we were hanging round the river and it was Dark Jules (who, it turned out, did piss in his bed) who spotted the smoke while he was coming away from the shower-block. As he ran

towards the tent, it burst into flames and he was yelling and yelling. He got there first and ran into the tent and grabbed our stuff and threw it out into the vines, went in and grabbed some more, threw that, and so by the time we got there he was crying and choking but he had saved a load of our stuff. Soon, Henri the *moniteur* had a chain set up and we were hurling water at it, and I was thinking about the praying mantis, *la mante religieuse*, burned at the stake, and hours later, sitting under the fig tree Pink Nicolas said that Dark Jules's sheet hadn't burned and the girls told Pink Nicolas that he was a shit and smacked him hard.

Mme Goetschy's husband turned up and said that
the boys from the union at Berliet would be joining
us. Berliet, the truck factory. That was why Lucien
le blond turned up along with two tall white boys,
Bernard *et* Bertrand. Lucien was white too but that
was because he was nearly albino. White wavy hair
that he was always patting, and white hairs on his
legs. He said he had won the Marseille under-seventeen
two hundred metres. He wore running shorts, and once
when we camped out by the side of the river he danced
in front of everybody singing Little Richard's
'Balambambula tooty frooty' as if it was French. He
liked the way his legs moved. When we were up
on the plateau in the heavy heat, he got thirsty but
I had brought my dad's US Army water bottle.
– Let me have a drink, he said.
– Hang on, I said.
– You shit, he said, call yourself a Communist and
    you can't share your water?
And he rammed the metal spout into my teeth.

Bernard *et* Bertrand said that they were the kind of guys who like to do things and Benzizi looked round at everyone. Bernard *et* Bertrand would have to learn that when it came to doing things they should talk to Benzizi first. They organized the building of a ford. Every day, we lifted rocks and boulders and laid them in the river. I had never sweated like it. M. Goetschy came and stood on the bank and saw my back looking up at the sun.

– *Jolie écrevisse!* he called out, pretty lobster!
We moved hundreds of stones. Henri loved it, he called us *bagnards*, hard-labour convicts, and sang '*Merde à Vauban*' at us. Goddemarre said, *Qu'est-ce que c'est, ce bouleau*? One day, after moving more boulders, we sat down to eat, and I think Henri said something about how maybe even if we finished the ford, we probably wouldn't be able to get cars over it and Bernard exploded. He shouted about how it had been his idea and that we hadn't helped him, and Henri had never taken it seriously and we could all go fuck ourselves and he was fucked if he was going to eat the rest of his dinner. Bertrand, who was the only French boy in shorts I had ever seen with socks on, put his arm round him but Bernard shrugged it off. I said if

he wasn't eating his ice cream, I would have it and I pulled his plate over and sat eating his ice cream. Benzizi and Goddemarre and Pink Nicolas and Maurice the footballer and Alain the trainee electrician looked at me. I went on eating the ice cream.

– Benzizi said, we don't do that sort of thing, Mike.

It was Bernard who tried to lead the lentil strike.
He said that he didn't want to eat peasants' food.
Every Thursday we had lentils. We didn't cook
our own food; two women from the village came
in and they brought Michel, a son of one of them.
He looked as if his body was held together by
wires. Under the skin all over him, you could see
the wires pulling on his bones. He took two of us
down to the cellars and showed us how we could
steal the *moniteurs'* wine. He opened a bottle and
gave it to us. I said that I didn't believe it was wine,
he was just trying to trick me.

— It's vinegar, I said.

He loved that.

— Mike says it's vinegar. Look, he said, watch me,
and he lifted the bottle in its straw casing up to his
mouth and gulped it down.

— Now you have some.

Alain the trainee electrician and Benzizi joined in.

— No, I said, I think it's vinegar.

— Would I drink vinegar? he said.

— Perhaps, I said, if you wanted to trick me.

He loved that too. He took us to see the man the
boys called the Peasant and this old man gave us

pastis, with a thick aniseed smell, green Pernod
that he made himself. Bernard wanted that. He
drank it like it was milk and he went red and stupid
in a moment. The Peasant sat on his terrace
underneath his fig tree, drinking it every evening,
nodding to us as we mooched past him down below.
Michel often ate with us, and he loved the lentils. I
asked them once if Michel was a peasant and they
said yes but he was a good bloke, *un brave type*.
Even so, Bernard wouldn't eat lentils, and tried to
get us all to join the lentil strike. Some agreed,
especially Nicole in her three blue hankies. She
said that their parents didn't think their trade union
was sending them away to have lentils every
Thursday. I said I liked lentils. I loved their rough
brown taste and their thick sauce, with bits of old
burnt bacon (was it?) floating around. They asked me
if I ate lentils in England and I said I had never
seen them before.

– There you are, they said to Henri the
    moniteur, they don't eat them in England.
But they could hear me and Michel sucking them
in off our spoons.

Henri said that tonight we were going to
go up on the plateau and walk all night. We
crossed the river in the dark but there was
enough light from the stars for us to see
ourselves in the river. Up on the plateau we
saw glow-worms and toads; we alerted dogs
and got lost.

– We'll make a fire, said Henri.

So we made a fire and we cooked *petits pois
et lardons*; he stamped on the flames to turn
the wood to embers and threw strips of meat on
them. We sat under a bluey-white roadside light,
eating. Nicole and Giselle said that we would
never get back to the camp and everyone asked
Henri if he knew where we were.

– No, he said, so let's go.

A few hundred yards down the road he stopped.
He got out his torch and shone it on a stone by
the side of the road. There was a list of names.
Henri said that there had been a village here and
during the war the Nazis had killed all the men
of the village.

– Bastards, said Benzizi.

– *Dégueulasses*, said Alain the trainee
electrician.

We stood in the road, above us a huge sky,
the one or two trees watching us, Henri
at one end of a beam of light and the men's
names on the other. I tried asking Henri what
had happened but he couldn't speak and
Benzizi put his hand on my arm to shut me up.

I needed them more than they needed me. They
knew each other, their mothers and fathers worked
together, they shared the same schools and streets
and shops. They talked about meeting in the market.
I wanted to be them but I was irritated that I wasn't
them. There didn't seem to be anything they wanted
from me or anyone English that they wanted to know
about, or any English words that they wanted to hear.
They didn't need to know about houses with their eyes
shut, or why it got up my nose that the deputy head
had told me that her idea of the ideal grammar
school pupil was one who conforms and why the
ones who didn't, discovered Charlie Parker. My
currency was valueless. The joke about Hymie and
the Red Cross didn't translate; my imitation of our
biology teacher or *Danger Man* from weekend TV
didn't work. No one needed to care about even the
tiniest fragment of cricket or Arsenal. There was a time
when someone asked me something about Prince
Charles but I said that I was a republican, which set
up a running gag: every other day someone sitting
near me would sing: 'Godde sev ze quinne' and leap
to their feet. I said that I thought Brigitte Bardot was
incroyable because the previous year I had seen her

projected on to a wall in the village square down the
road from here; babies crying, children playing football,
when in the midst of the kerfuffle, up there on the wall
for all to see, framed by the café owner's washing, BB
took all her clothes off and lay down on her back on
a beach. And the old ladies in black, their husbands long
dead from the war, the old men who had just finished their
game of *boules* right where we were sitting, the young
women who were making plans for the fête next week, the
young men who knew that one day soon they would
have to leave this place for work in Clermont or Lyon,
all of them, the whole village, clapped to see Bardot show
herself to them right there on their wall.
– You know, I said, they cut that bit out when they
    showed it in England.
– Ah, that's you Anglo-Saxons again, said Henri
    the *moniteur*.
And I thought, what have the Anglo-Saxons got to do
with it? What's he on about? And anyway, *merde, je
suis pas anglo-saxon, moi, hein*? Shit, I'm not Anglo-Saxon,
me, OK?

In the wood across the river the rocks turned
into a cliff. In amongst these was a cave. The
Grotte du soldat, they called it, because during
the war, which, after all, had ended only
seventeen years earlier, a man from the
Resistance had hidden in it. We went in with
torches, the cool smacking our faces; the heat
hugging us when we came out. I often did the
trip inside with Pink Nicolas. Like me, he seemed
to want the blackness beyond the pool of torch-
light. There was a cliff about twice our height that
we had to climb up. At the top, we had to lie down
and squeeze under a rock to get into the next
chamber and there was a moment when you weren't
holding on to anything; the rock seemed to weigh
down on your chest in the dark, while you remembered,
but couldn't see, the cliff below. Once Pink Nicolas
and me moved around the chamber for too long and
we couldn't find our way back to the cliff. In seconds,
every metre in front of us was new and the torchlight
wasn't strong enough to light up the chamber. We
thought that we'd find the cliff by moving to the
right, thinking we were making a circle. We didn't,
and it seemed like we were going further into the

chamber where we'd never been before. Pink
Nicolas said that we should turn the torches out to
see if we could see light. For a moment we stood
in the cold blackness, listening to our breathing.
Then we turned them back on and walked over
the damp rocks some more, till we heard Benzizi
shouting that it was time for lunch,
– *Putain*, where the fuck are you?
– Pink Nicolas whispered to me quick, Don't
  ever tell them that we were lost.

Two days later, me and Lucien le blond were standing in the river throwing stones when Françoise came running out of the woods.
– Didi, she screamed.
Didi with his thick, knotty legs was Mme Goetschy's brother-in-law and a *moniteur* for the little ones.
– He's fallen in the cave and he's not moving, he's lying in the cave, not moving. *Il bouge pas.*
I knew where he must have fallen. Down the cliff. Lucien didn't wait to wonder, he started running. He splashed out of the water and headed for the office and shower-block. I was caught, should I go to the cave or follow Lucien? The way to the office was rocky, what if he broke his ankle? I ran after him. By the time I got near the building, people were running back towards me with blankets and medics had been called, Mme Goetschy's sister was sobbing with big sad sobs. They found him lying on his back, his skull cracked. There was a moment when we saw him as they loaded him on to the chariot over the river, his brown skin turned to khaki. I asked Françoise if it happened

by the cliff, but she had no idea what I was talking about.

– Why did you run after Lucien instead of going back to the cave?

There was a tree I found where a cicada laughed all summer and the fat red ants worked on me and my feet. It stood on its own by the side of the stone path running from the shower-block to the river. There were times there, on my own too, that I let myself go back to the last day; the coach home from the day trip to Coventry when we knew that this was the last time together. Five years over, and now one of us was off, he said, to be a fridge mechanic, one a travel agent, another to art school; secretaries, hairdressers and more study. As the bus pointed towards London and night came down, we were passengers on a boat that we couldn't stop, singing and drinking goodbye. So we reached for each other, touching and daring what had never been tried before. The boat stopped, we climbed out and went off, this way and that, in ones and twos down the long roads of shut-eyed houses. Under the cicada, I wrote someone a letter saying that I couldn't go on with all that, with any of that.

The scorpion man arrived one afternoon when
the heat was in our eyes. He wore brown English-style
shorts (the first I had seen for weeks), a used
vest and something like a cowboy hat, sweat-stained
round his hairline. His eyes were veiled with tinted
glasses and his skin was as dark as it's possible for
someone I called white. I liked his ancient sandals.
He said that he would look for scorpions and right
where we walked every day between the tents, round
the bottom of the stairs leading to the office in the
alleyway between the shower-block and the peasant's
house, he paced about, lifting stones. We followed after
until he said in a quiet voice: '*Voilà!*' We moved in
and watched him shunt something into a polythene wallet.
Its tail lifted and wagged.
– And there's the sac of poison, he said.
It seemed so well made. A hook to stick in and
catch your skin, with its ammo-store of killer-liquid
tucked in just behind, ready to pour in through the
hole it had made in you.
– No worse than a wasp sting, this one,
    he said.
We knew about that. One night in a barn that a farmer
let us sleep in, Alain started shouting that a scorpion

61

had got him. The torches went on, everyone laughing
at Alain and his alarms.
— Look, he said, and there was
    something like a pimple on his rib.
— It's a pimple, Alain, we said.
— But a few seconds later he shouted,
    Et putain, what's this, then?
And it was a scorpion, scrabbling about on the barn
floor where we had all been sleeping. It just so
happened that it was Alain it punctured first, Alain
the trainee electrician who fitted the bulbs for the
outdoor lights, Alain who would say to me at least
three times a day:
— *Les anglais avec le marché commun –*
    déguelasses, the English with the
    Common Market – disgusting;
    which as far as I knew seemed likely but,
    whatever the truth, I loved saying it with
    him, in chorus.

I don't speak English. I don't even speak the
French I was taught. Shoes aren't *les chaussures*
here. They're *les goddasses*, *l'eau* is *la flotte*,
le vin is *le pinard*. My head is inside out;
English used to be in deep and French outside.
I've stopped translating. I don't think 'let's go'
and turn it into *on y va*. *On y va* is all I've got.
And it's the same with *j'en sais rien, moi,* and
n'y'en a plus and *ça y est*. I don't know what
the English is doing. I think it's dying. The
French is pushing it out of its seat in the middle
where it thought it was safe. It thought it was in
charge and now it isn't.

With ten days to go before the end, M. Goetschy came to us and said that we would go on a canoe trip for several days, down the Ardèche from Pont d'Arc to the Rhône. I thought he meant kayaks but a day later a truck arrived and we unloaded fat-bellied wooden canoes. One of us sat in the front pulling, while the one in the back had to both pull and control. He trained us on the horseshoe of our river, shouting, *appel*, *écarte*, teaching the one in the back to do what I thought only Hiawatha knew: how to paddle a canoe on your own. Only boys could do this, he said, and Nicole spat into the river and said they could have done it, *merde*. We fanned out on to the river at Pont d'Arc, and we're paddling, shouted Goetschy to us, under this, the biggest natural bridge in Europe, boys. I was with Bernard and we were the last in the line of ten red canoes pushing along on water that glittered in our faces. We called out to each other, and our voices bounced down the gorge. At La Chaise we tried to handle white water with our paddles buried in the foam. At night we slept on thyme and sucked Mont Blanc condensed milk out of tubes that looked like they ought to be full of toothpaste. Coming round one cliff, two naked women kneeling up in a canoe skimmed towards us. Keep your eyes on the river, shouted Goetschy and laughed into the air. And later we sat under the Cathédrale, a pinnacle of rock, three or four hundred feet above us, with three spires and an eagle prowling round. Bernard, giggling during his turn in the back, levered his paddle against a rock and snapped it. For the last five miles to the Rhône, he had my paddle and I lay in the belly of the canoe taking the sun full on, like, I thought, a sahib. Lucien le blond cursed my luck. When we arrived back at the *colonie*, the girls seemed to know that they should be there to meet us, and they told us how brown we were and we showed them our blisters and they went back to their Nivea and adjusting each other. They had become even more beautiful and unbearable, the way their arms reached forward and away from their bodies making a space that we were never in.

I was never sure whose idea it was to invade their tent. The plan was that we would come down off our vine terrace, cross the field and get down to the bamboo copse by the river which sheltered the girls' tent. It had to be secret and the plan was whispered all day. We would go after *le repas* in the dark, when the *moniteurs* sat in the office, drinking wine, as the mosquitoes and moths fried themselves on the purple killer light. They would think we were under the fig trees talking about Les Platters but we would be flying across the field to the girls' tent.

– Are you with us, Mike? they said.

I wasn't sure what I was with or what I was against. What were we going to do when we got there? What were we going to say that we didn't say when we were with them? Benzizi said that he was going to tell Françoise that she was a beautiful woman. Bernard said that he thought Nicole was the best and Dark Jules kept saying, Giselle, Giselle, and shaking his head. We crept away from the fig trees, round to the vine-terrace, and then across the field. At night it was clearer that the horseshoe of the river sat under

a high circle of cliff. It was cowboy country.
There were about fifteen of us, hopping over the
rocks and thistles, swearing as our toes scraped
the stones. And then we got to the bamboo: their
settlement, with their washing lines hung with
their jeans and T-shirts. The light was on inside the
tent but it was quiet. Not a sound. We looked at
each other. What was the plan? That we would
rush the tent? Then what? Benzizi pointed to the
path through the bamboo and we tiptoed along it
and just where it opened out into the space in
front of the tent, we saw that Henri and Mme
Goetschy were sitting, waiting for us.

– *Salut*, said Henri. His face was lined
   with false smiles. What a good evening
   for a hike. You should have told me
   that you fancied one more before
   the end of the *colonie*. We could have
   gone up on the plateau again.

Mme Goetschy said that it was sad, sad, sad. Soon
everyone would be back in Lyon, back at school, the
colonie would be finished. Let's not have a sad end.

In the coach back to Lyon, Nicole cried and cried and cried. Maurice sang, *Allez l'O. L, allez l'O. L. Allez.* Coming down off the mountains, Benzizi shouted that the coach was on fire. We looked down and the wooden floor was burning. There were flames round the bottom of Pink Nicolas' seat. The coach driver stopped the coach and pushed his way towards us. He waved his hand and said it wasn't a big thing, *pas grand' chose.* He stamped on the wooden floor and the flames went out under his foot and off we went. As we got into Lyon, they started cheering and the coach pulled up under the walls of Gerland, the chemical works. Some of their parents were there. Not Goddemarre's, not Benzizi's, not Alain the trainee electrician's. They were men now. I shook everyone's hand. Let's write, we said. Mme Goetschy said that she would take me to the station, the Gare de Lyon.

– You call Lyon station the Gare de Lyon? I said.

– Of course, she said.

After a while, I said,

– And when you rang the Gare de Lyon
about my anorak and the wallet, did you
ring this Gare de Lyon or the Gare de
Lyon in Paris?

– Oh, this one of course, she said.

At the station she hugged me and kissed me and said that it had been a good *colonie*. And I nodded and nodded and because I couldn't say it all, I couldn't say any of it and then she was gone.

My brother and father were waiting for me at Waterloo. In the end, you wrote good letters, he said. We started to get the picture. You're not as brown as I thought you'd be. Did it rain? No, I said, it didn't rain once. For the whole six weeks we had sun. I got into the car, my brother sat in the front and I sat in the back. Don't you want to know your exam results? my father asked. He told me. I looked at London. So what do you think? he said. Not bad, I said. Not bad? he said. Not one 'A'. Not even for English Literature. My brother was killing himself sitting in the front. He had been there before. The results inquest. How he loved it now that it was me in the dock. He sat there mouthing: not one 'A', shaking his head, doing the sad disbelief thing, creasing his cheek like our father did and then looking back at me and laughing and laughing. Have you got a present for your mother? my father said. Have you got a present for your mother? said my brother.

– I want to be a doctor.

It must have sounded sweeter than Mozart.
Instead of taking up with the things that had
mattered to them – the deaths of Mercutio and
Cleopatra; the trial of Sacco and Vanzetti,
Robeson singing 'Joe Hill'; *Great Expectations*,
Catch-22 and the language of seven-year-olds;
instead of reading books about books about
books, I would do something real. A doctor.
Wasn't there a gallery of good people who
came out of the East End who were all
doctors? Kipper Harvey, Harry Barst, Chick
Carter, Betty Fisher? That's what a good
Jewish socialist should do – become a doctor.
And now I had said I wanted to be one. No
matter that I hadn't done any physics or
chemistry since I was twelve, no matter that I
liked sitting in my bedroom trying to be D. H.
Lawrence. It could all be managed. I could
even carry on doing *Garibaldi* and *Candide*
and *Nostromo* and do all that science stuff
later at medical school. We've talked to Chick,
they said. It's called First M.B. I hoped, like
you hope when you leap across a stream, that
First M. B. would include scorpions.

I got a card. All it said was:
– *Les anglais avec le marché commun –*
  déguelasses.

We were evicted from our flat. A man who
looked like Danny Kaye bought the building,
sold baby clothes in Babettes, his shop on the
ground floor beneath us. He cleared us out.
He tried to be nice about it by saying that he
wanted us to stay and it was only his lawyers
who were giving us the heave-ho. On my last
day in my bedroom I lay on my back and
wrote 'Fuck off Babette' on the underside of
the metal mantelpiece. It meant a new school,
the different world of a single-sex, town grammar,
founded two hundred and fifty years earlier by
a Protestant brewer. A group of them talked like
I was the first Jew they had ever met, and so for
a while they wanted me to be the kind they thought
they knew. If one of them dropped a coin by mistake
on the floor they would shout, don't throw your
money about when he's there; or, better still, one
of them would *throw* a coin down and say,
watch him, he'll be the first to go for it. I helped out
by putting on what I thought they thought was a
Jewish accent. That way we could all get on.
Another group came over to the house, and they
asked me what all my parents' books were for

but together we got into Big Bill Broonzy, Sonny
Terry and Brownie McGhee, Woody Guthrie and
Dylan – or Robert Zimmerman, as it told us on the
cover. They asked me if that meant he was one too
and I said yes, but then, I thought, so was Babette,
though I didn't say so. I bought a harmonica and
tried to play it like Sonny Terry:

> Down in the henhouse on my knees, I
> thought I heard a chicken sneeze. Only
> the rooster sayin his prayers, thankin
> god the hen's upstairs . . . We shall be
> free, in the mornin, we shall be free
> wooo wooo

As we unpacked *Candide* each week, it
emerged as perfect. What made it so like a
present was the way Voltaire gave us the
chance to make each line mean the opposite
of what it said. He became a friend of ours.
He noticed that kings command massacres.
In the midst of one, the tragedy of one of the
castrati had us creased up: ten seventeen-year-
old boys in black-and-green school uniform,
too big for the desks in Room 14, rain outside,
Mr Emmans waving his hands: *O che sciagura
d'essere senza coglioni*, Voltaire has the man
speaking Italian, 'O what agony it is to be
without bollocks.' A few weeks later I was in
hospital. When a car had hit me, my pelvis had
come apart. All ten of the *Candide* class came
to see me, strung up in a pelvis-hammock,
along with all twenty of the rugby squad, all
thirty of the cast and crew of *Twelfth Night* apart
from the guy who was due to play Belch. He was
lying in the bed looking at them all and thanking
for them being so worried and kind.
– What's it like in here? they asked.
– Him over there, I said, is a First
    World War hero. He's in here because his

bladder's packed up. He told us the one
about how everyone's a friend in
the army now. Call everyone 'chum'.
Right up from the sergeant-major
to the brigadier-general. The new
recruit's impressed. He says to the
Colonel, so if we all call you 'chum'
what do you call the likes of us?
what do you call your privates? I
call 'em the same as you call 'em,
son, says the colonel. I call 'em
bollocks.
– And what about him over there?
– Oh him and him and him they're all
motorbike boys, they've lost their
legs. Him over there got so desperate
to see his girlfriend, they let him go
home for the weekend. The reason
why he's looking worried, is that
she's pregnant. He keeps singing
that Frank Ifield song: 'Don't blame
Me'. The First World War hero says
to him, there ain't anyone else to
blame, sonny. Hey but listen I'm

in trouble. Every morning at six when
it's still dark an Italian cleaner comes in.
I had been saying hello to her for a few
days until one morning, I leaned out of
the bed, and let's face it she doesn't know
why I've got this hammock round my
middle, and I moaned out: *O che sciagura
d'essere senza coglioni*. I thought she'd
think it was funny, but she ran out the
ward screaming. The sister came running
in and shouted at me: What have you
been saying to my cleaners? If you've
said anything rude or improper, I shall
throw you out of this hospital. So I
said that I didn't know what it meant.
It was just a line in a famous, classic
French book that we're reading for
A-level but because it was in Italian
I didn't know what it meant . . . She
said that she didn't believe a word
I was saying, that if I said anything
at all that offended any of her cleaners
or nurses she would do just as she said
and throw me out. Then off she went

and the motorbike boys all said, what did you say? What did you say? So I told them but it was on condition that they didn't tell Sister that I did know what it meant. And they didn't say a word.

I planned my escape as I stood dissecting
out the thyroid gland of a rat. I wasn't
someone who loved cranial nerves. I learnt
how to recite acromio trapezius, acromio
deltoid, with a guy who said he had done
philosophy at the Sorbonne, written a novel
about a plot to assassinate de Gaulle, and
was paying for his medical course by running
a caff in Walthamstow market where the
Krays liked to go for omelette and chips. The
novel had got him into trouble with ex-ministers
in the de Gaulle government, and one of them,
Jacques Soustelle, was, he said, suing him for
libel. He called me 'The Stalinist' and told me
about a woman who had known Kafka's
mistress and who had spent the war in two
concentration camps, one in Russia, one in
Germany. It was more interesting than the
carotid artery. The doctors' sons seemed to
think that anything in the world was more
interesting than the carotid artery but it didn't
bother them like it bothered me. They just went
on filling fathers' shoes. I got out by getting in
somewhere else.

The somewhere else was a place founded,
they told us, by Protestant Nonconformists,
and their chapel was for my use. I stayed
up late and talked outside someone's window.
A small stoat, a world expert in something
Latin, summoned me. He said that behaviour
like this warranted a fine, old chap. A few days
later, a group of people celebrated winning
something. They shouted around the Protestant
Nonconformist structures for most of a night,
removed a toilet and dropped it in a flower bed.
I made the mistake of asking the stoat if this was
something that he dealt with too and if not,
could I have my money back? He wrote back
to explain that I was learning a lesson in how
justice is dispensed.

I was now on humans. Six of us used our
scalpels to find out what an old woman
was made of. One of us came from Ilkley.
He dropped the woman's lower arm
on me and said, 'Do you want a hand?'
Like the others, I talked of the woman as
'my body'. 'Excuse me, sir, shall I cover up
my body now?' The guy from Ilkley said,
'Let's call her Gladys.' And it was him who
noticed that the reason why we were doing
the Lloyd disassociation test on the Lloyd
apparatus was because the bloke teaching
us was Lloyd, and the tiny little smiley
bloke with a Czech accent who came round
the lab was Krebs.
– Krebs?
– Krebs Cycle, we did it last week.
– Did we?

Whether it was the grammar school boy from Sunderland whose dad worked at Courtauld's and who said that every Saturday he stood at Roker Park and got meat pies chucked at the back of his head or the one from the admiral's family who smoked a pipe and did Latin, or the one from Sedbergh who wore a waistcoat and did sherry, or the fierce little Jewish one with glasses who said she wanted to be a psychiatrist, or the laid-back one in velvet trousers who had been to a school that had its own theatre and kiln and in-house composer, or all of them, I didn't get it. Or it didn't translate. Or I didn't or couldn't or wouldn't translate: the Big Rock Candy Mountain, or Benzizi, Aldermaston, Babette, *O che sciagura, Herrel shmerel.*

So I tried to detach. My parents were
desolate. Surely I wasn't going to
end up doing what they did? Books,
and books about books, and teaching
people about books about books? I
said that sounded good enough for me.
The change would have to be managed
by a famous small man with a giant
voice and no neck called the warden.
He had once written a book called
Primitive Song and when he spoke
his voice rolled out in bass punches
till the last syllable of a sentence when
for no obvious reason, it dipped,
paused mid-syllable and then rose. I
rang him.
– Bowra-[pause]-a
– Michael Rosen here, could I
    come and see y–
– Four o'clock tomorro-ow
My father thought he'd better show
up to prove that he was going along
with this appalling idea. We arrived,
nothing was said on the way in. We

sat down. No papers appeared. We
were in our coats. The meeting
began.
– Mm?
– I would like to change course.
– From what to wha-at?
– Medicine to English.
– Can you write a sente-ence?
– I think s–
He turned to my father.
– What do you think of thi-is?
My father had prepared a five-minute speech:
– I think that it's a good –
– Splendid – convince your father,
    convince anyo-one. Haven't got
    any money to help you ou-out.
    Fifty pounds that's a-all. Bye.
And that was it; in less than three minutes
I was back to books, and books about
books.

Some superstoats banned the newspaper. The
editors were cross but said they didn't think they
ought to do anything. I stood at a Gestetner machine
turning out leaflets, posters were coming in from
Paris: *Sous le pavé, la plage*, beneath the cobbles
the beach; we marched to the stoats' office, they
took no notice, Someone chalked up: 'Deanz means
finez'; Agent Orange was falling and falling; the
stoats banned leafleting and it wasn't long before
their iron gates were being pushed in, and we were
through, first in: Trevor the Jamaican, and then Attar
from Pakistan. On the other side of the road little
Bob Reich was explaining why he agreed with the
Principle but disagreed with the process. Bowra said
they wanted me out, I had offended too many people,
write an apology-y. I wrote that I was sorry that I had
personalized the attack. He looked at the letter and
said, You haven't apologized at a-all. Very clever-er.
I like it. It'll keep them quie-et. Now do me the favour
of doing some wo-ork. The halls were filling with
people who wanted to go to Grosvenor Square; in
London a worker from Renault Bilancourt told us that
there had to be more to life than *ce bouleau*, we aren't
slaves, so we occupied. Not even the CRS would touch us.

Paris, Lyon, Marseille, everywhere. I thought about
Gerland and Benzizi. At Grosvenor Square we were
upended and carried off. I noticed that all they put on
the charge sheet for me was 'big'. No one ID'd me so
they kept us in Savile Row to sing and clap till three in the
morning. Strangers were friends. Outside, my father
and brother were waiting for me, my brother sat in the
front, I sat in the back. They can't ignore this one, my
father said. The streets were so full Wilson didn't send
one soldier, but the faculty said that it was out of the
question for them to change the syllabus. Worki-ing?
said Bowra. No, not really, I said. Thinki-ing? said
Bowra. No, not really, I said. Mm, he said, I've completely
lost the capacity to do either-er. When the exam came they
hovered in their gowns in case there was a riot. There
wasn't. I didn't feel like wearing the obligatory flower.
I wore a badge saying A Carnation, and painted Jeff
Chaucer on my back. Then Trevor said, today we fight
the colour bar, and he had us sitting in, in a hairdresser's
who wouldn't cut his girlfriend's hair. Off to the cells
again, more singing and clapping. Strangers were friends.
In court we strung it out for hours, claiming that it wasn't
us who had begun this obstruction business, it was the
hairdresser obstructing people from having their

hair cut. Then it was all over and we were supposed to go off and carry on with the rest of our lives. I heard that they changed the syllabus about the same time as Kissinger prevented peace or Nixon begged for it, the rumour went round that Trevor had gone home and made for the hills with the guys and I read in the paper that Bowra died. I remembered that Bowra had once said to me: Bertie Russell met Lenin, you know, and Bertie asked Lenin, what do you do with the aristocracy now that the revolution has come, Lenin? And Lenin said to Bertie, we string them up from the nearest tree. Bertie didn't like Leni-in, Bowra said.

There were about four of us in a room with a baby. We were all men. None of the men was the baby's father. The baby's mother and her friends had invited us over and then popped out. For a moment. For three hours we were trying to look after the baby. None of us had done nappies. Or bottles. Or baby food. We did OK. Then the women came back. It was an experiment, they said.

Mrs Previser had covered her walls with photos. Some in frames, some stuck there with tape, some propped up on dressers and sideboards. I looked into the people's faces. Portraits, couples, group shots, families, football teams, men in uniform, coronations. 'You're looking at the photos,' she said. 'Yes. . . . A lot of memories here,' I said. 'No,' she said, 'I don't know any of them.' I went on looking. 'None of them?' 'No,' she said, 'they're just photos I find. I've got hundreds more over there.' 'You don't know any of these people?' 'Not one.' 'So what about your relatives?' 'Oh there's no point in my having photos of them. I can remember them.' She sounded contemptuous. 'I've got all these because no one knows them. If it wasn't for me, they'd all be gone.' 'Maybe there are people somewhere who remember them?' 'No, these aren't lost photos. They're all from second-hand shops. They're photos that people didn't want.'

Sometimes you're not at home when you're at home; where what you belong to is what you don't belong to; there's no reason to stay, so you stay; being unhappy feels bad, so carrying on being unhappy feels OK; you get good at complaining about it, so you do nothing; you don't do anything nasty to yourself, so you do it to someone else instead; and that vanishes it. You're living in another place.

It didn't seem possible that every day a building
worker was killed. The man went up on a scaffold
and showed us how you could rig it without doing
it by the book. If you do it on the lump, he said,
it's the subbie who takes you on; you come in, do it
and get out. Watch this, he said and he kicked a bolt
off the boards from three floors up and when it hit
the ground it buried itself in the mud. I remembered
being thirty feet up on a plank with no railings, painting
the ceiling of a factory. Holiday work, taken on by a
subbie. The bosses don't want the union coming in
and saying that you got to have rails, or you got to
have more boards. It's just a waste of money to them.
That's why we all come out and that's why they got
Dezzy, Ricky and the rest and banged them up. I sat
in the courtroom while the Crown proved that Warren
and Tomlinson were the violent ones and all this stuff
about scaffolding was neither here nor there. Their point
was that when people go to work, they should always
have the freedom to be killed. Jeff said the film that we
were giving to the union needed one more shot. We
drove down a lane and got to a wall. Jeff put the tripod
on the roof of the Land Rover and put the big lens on. He
zoomed in on what looked like a white palace, surrounded
by trees. The MacAlpines live here, he said.

I carried it everywhere. The persistent pain of
it stayed with me through washing-up; an
archipelago, he called it, not the Penal Colony.
More like an ocean, then, so wide and so deep,
a misery that I could hold only by keeping the
book in my bag. This was immense. And took us
beyond any possible excuse. And then the tanks.
We see them in black and white no worse than
beetles scrabbling across the steppes. They came
after the hunger and the round-ups and the slavery
and the slaughters. And in the middle of it, bands
of gunmen criss-crossing between the two phalanxes.
Reading this between washing the plates and
drying them, how would you like to be killed? From
cold? Blood giving up on the idea of moving. From
hunger? Gut-linings grinding on each other. Or would
you like to choose your bullet? From your countrymen,
from the enemy of your countrymen, or from the
enemy of the enemy of your countrymen? Here's a
gun. If you use it you will die. If you don't, you will
die. Ah, you've survived. Then you're a traitor and
must die. So, here and in France and everywhere,
editors and general secretaries and executive members
you knew and you lied. And in so doing sent the words

of the Commune down the sink. People think they're
poison in our mouths.

The sound of those Irish pipes could do
things to the insides of your muscles.
Pat McCarthy from Galway told me
he played them every day of the week.
He had been on a tour to the States last
April. I imagined him wowing Irish-Americans
with that rough edgy sound.
You could think that it was calling out to
you. They have a terrible nigger problem
over there, he said. That'll be a bit like
the paddy problem we have over here
then, I said. And haven't you made a
particular kind of point there? he said.

Hundreds turned up. There were people here I had never seen. She had been theirs too, had she? And they had been hers? This is a life? People come dressed like they never dress; people who usually walk in straight lines walking round and about. But hundreds. So she was part of a lot. There were people here, strangers, who had believed in her.

It was in an office that I overheard a woman saying that she hated council flats and tower blocks. But it wasn't the architecture, it was the people. Out there, on the other side of this window, her line was that it was bad. People were bad. In here we were OK. But if you were with her on your own, meeting her, one by one, then for her the others in here were bad too. So we were all bad. That only left her who was good.

Within days, it seems that they were out on the streets selling a penny sheet that told it as a story: 'An account of the court martial, sentence and execution of Richard Parker for Mutiny held on board His Majesty's ship the NEPTUNE, lying in the river Thames, Greenhithe.' It said that the 'prisoner was charged with making, and having endeavoured to make, a mutiny among the seamen of His Majesty's ships at the Nore; with having caused assemblies of these seamen to meet frequently, and with having behaved himself contemptuously toward and disobeyed his officers.' This, I remembered, was the man who had helped start the 'floating parliament' and who said, 'How could I indifferently stand by, and behold some of the very best of my fellow-creatures cruelly treated by some of the very worst?' So, on Friday 30 June 1797 at eight o'clock in the morning, they hung him up in front of thousands of seamen and shot him. 'He was interred exactly at noon,' it says, but then adds: 'His body was afterward secretly taken up, and conveyed to London, and decently interred in Whitechapel church yard.' Alongside this there's a song, called 'The Death of Parker', written as if sung by his widow: 'For by the death of my brave Parker/Fortune has proved to me unkind,/Tho' doom'd by law he was to suffer/I can't erase him from my mind.' I wondered about that business of being secretly taken up and interred in Whitechapel. I went down there but Whitechapel church was bombed flat and the churchyard is a little park where winos were laid out in the sun. A few gravestones stand round the edges. But a burial is a burial so I went to the Central Library and looked up the burial records for June 1797: 'Thomas Gregg, Workhouse, 50, Decline; Joseph Matthews, Red Lion Street, 26, Thrush; Jane Bright, Petticoat Lane, 45, Decline; Elizabeth Trundell, Greyhound Lane, 22, Asthma; Richard Parker, Sheerness, Kent, 33, Execution'. And underneath, the clerk had written, 'This was Parker, the President of the mutinous Delegates on board the fleet at the Nore. He was hanged on board the HMS Sandwich on the 30th day of June.' And then the list goes on: 'Richard Stock, Leman Street, 26, Fever; Mary Clark, Colchester Street, 31, Decline . . .' I wondered about who it was who could have taken Parker's body from Greenhithe to Whitechapel, and what kind of vicar broke the law to allow a mutineer to be buried in his churchyard. They put a hood over his head when they strung him up. It was a way of snuffing him out, I suppose. On 11 May 1905, Mr W. Rundle, the landlord of the Farmers' Inn, St Merryn, near Wadebridge in Cornwall, was heard singing a 'Death of Parker' song. A Mrs Barnes was singing it nearby, and in May

1907 someone else was singing it in Hannington, Kingsclere, Hampshire: '"Twas by the death of my brave Parker/Fortune proved to me unkind,/Although Parker was hung for mutiny/Worse than him was left behind./I thought I saw the yellow flag flying/In token for my husband to die,/A gun was fired, which was required/To hang him from the gallows tree.'

On the water across from where Grace Darling
saved all those people, our boat stopped.
It swayed on the sea, the chug-chug-chug
gone. The man in the hat came out of his
little upright house and climbed over us to get
to the mid-point. Right there, a small Hassidic
boy in his *kapel* and *peyes* was holding on
to a lever the size of a fence post. He had
got interested in it and pulled it. This had
turned the engine off. The man in the hat
pushed the lever back and climbed over us
to get back to his upright house. Everyone
looked at the boy. The boat started up again
and we were soon at the place where Grace
Darling saved all those people.

As part of their programme of sticking up for human rights, the British National Party held a meeting at our school. They couldn't get in at first because hundreds of us met outside. The police spent an hour trying to push us out the way but in the end it turned out to be a bit easier for them to go round the back and smash in a door for them to go through. When we said that we would all like to attend the meeting they said that this might constitute a danger to public safety so they only let twenty of us in. After a few minutes, the speakers called on their helpers to turn their Union Jack poles with brass points into spears and they ran at us. When we got outside, the police started arresting us. On the way home, they arrested some Bangladeshi boys whose younger brothers and sisters went to the school.

There were times when I was on my own
in the studio late at night. Through the
glass the producer and the studio manager
talking to each other with no sound reaching
me. They told me I was recording for the
world. Reading words from inside a silent
room that could be heard anywhere. Someone
once told me that there used to be a swimming
pool in here and behind a curtain there was
a grand piano. Upstairs and outside, the buses
curved round the Aldwych or streamed up
Kingsway; theatres gobbled up queues. I was
talking about books. The two women behind
the glass moved like surgeons from console to
tape to deck. Great writers fell out of my
mouth. I coughed. Go back. Redo that para.
Centuries pass. Tom Paine, Amy Tan, that
sort of thing. And then nothing. I go into the
operating theatre. The surgeons look up and
nod. I back out. Don't want to breathe on the
tape. Coming out, I hope Security don't notice.
Oh no, they have. 'One moment, sir. Why have
you been in there?' 'I don't know.' Outside,
the buses are racing. The drivers know where

they're going. The 4 from Waterloo to Finsbury Park.

Thirty years later I arrived in the Ardèche with
my son and step-daughter. We drove down to the
turn on the road that led to the river. It's just down
here, I said. But it wasn't *just* down there. It was a
long way down and all along by the river on the
valley floor were campsites, the permanent kind,
with showers and shops. As we got near to the end
of the valley where I was waiting to see the horseshoe
and the cliffs I was gearing myself up that this too
would have its campsite selling *merguez et frites.*
But no, the tents ended and, just as it was, thirty years
before: nothing but the cliffs, the dust, the stones,
the scrub, a few vines, the heat in your eyes and the
river. Dad's going off on one, my son said. One wire
was there. Not two, no chariot. We can swim in this,
I said, and we can walk across. They didn't know why.
I had never said much about the *colonie*. It was
something in me. We swam across. I was shouting.
This is the terrace where our tent was. The house
where they set up an office was empty and beginning
to tumble. I pushed in an old door down below and the
pipes for the showers were still on the wall. The peasant's
house was going under creepers and out the back the
fig trees had spread wide and low. I tried to find the

path down to the bamboo copse but it was overgrown,
I found the way to the Grotte du Soldat but my kids said,
don't go in. We swam again in the river and I was glad
they were there to see it. I wasn't on my own. They
were nearly the same age as I was then. I wondered how
many of the *colonie* had kids. Had they brought them
here? Pink Nicolas, Goddemarre, Dark Jules, Bernard
et Bertrand, Françoise, Mme Goetschy, M. Goetschy,
Lucien le Blond, Maurice the footballer, Mme
Goetschy's sister and her husband, Nicole, Henri the
moniteur, Giselle, Alain the trainee electrician and
Benzizi. And Benzizi. Of course, Benzizi. Not one of them
had I ever seen again but all of them still there. *Merde à
Vauban.*

I thought I had lost them. One of them wasn't mine and the other was mine but I thought he didn't want to be. I thought I'd better take off before it got worse: the States, Ringelblum would put me up. France, I could buy a studio in Montparnasse for less than thirty grand. But they came over to see me: watch MTV, play football, take us to the Holloway Odeon, let's go to Brittany, we'll live with you half the time.

It didn't seem possible to solve things by doing nothing so I went to a flat on the second floor in Hammersmith The limescale in the bath was stained with iron. The trucks going west and east listened in. I said that I felt that I was losing things but that people thought they were losing me. Was that my problem or other people's problems? he said. I don't know, I said. It wasn't his job to tell me, he said, but how interesting that I had expressed it like that: as a problem. That's interesting? I said. There was my shower that needed fixing; is that a problem? I said. He couldn't say. It'll be a problem until the guy comes and fixes it, I said, he's not coming till next Tuesday. You keep saying the word 'fix', he said. Are you saying that I'm in a fix? I said. I'm not saying anything, he said. Or that I'm fixed in my ideas, I said. Who can say? he said. Or that I like things to feel fixed? Or that I get stuck on one thing? Fixed? It's you saying all these things, he said, not me. Excuse me, I said, have you got a book under the table? Sorry? he said. It seems like this conversation is going on while you're reading a book and you keep looking up the things I'm saying in an index at the back. Wouldn't it be easier to just tell me what you're looking up and read out what it says? Either that or just give me the book? I think you need to think why you imagine I have a book, he said. I don't need to think about that at all, I said. Then you don't understand how we can proceed, he said. Then I won't proceed, I said. That would be a mistake, he said. That's the first and only time you've expressed an opinion, I said, wouldn't you say that it was interesting? I don't think so, he said. And isn't it interesting that you've used the word 'mistake'? I can say, he said, that it's a mistake because we've barely scratched the surface here, we need to go deeper into the forest before we can get out of it.

When plumber Lee fitted me a pressure boiler
he told me that there'll be non-stop hot water.
When I stand in the shower, it's endless. I could
stay there for three hours or for three days and
the hot water would keep coming. I can look up
into the spray and it doesn't stop. The wet heat
pours on to my muscles. I hear myself sigh from
the depth of it. It never says that it'll only stay
hot if I'm good and it doesn't go cold if I get out;
it doesn't take itself off the wall and go; if I don't
shower for a couple of days, it's still hot when I
come back and it doesn't give a damn about what
I say or think or do.

I was sitting on the 253. The man across the aisle
was explaining to a woman that Jews eat people.
– I'm Jewish, I said, and I don't eat
    people. Look, I'm not eating you. I
    don't want to eat you.
He said, Don't you know your history?
    You should do some reading.

Our viruses and bacteria and fungal growths love us. They hurry between us like children running between houses in the city, slipping indoors, finding out the bedrooms and dens we've made for them. In a world of their own in a world of our own. They make us as they make us seep and itch; they're making us as we try to engulf them and expel them; as they blow our house down; what's mine is yours, what's yours is mine; can't live without them, can't live with them. Atishoo, atishoo he all falls down.

Hundreds of you turned up. I was a cork floating on you. Not a stone. Did I thank you for that? You made me bob. You were good.

The woman in the cemetery in Montparnasse
is crying and she's crying because her son has
died, he's died in an accident and she's brought
him flowers and she brings him flowers every
day and she looks at the photo on his grave
and when she looks at the photo she cries and
she cries and I say our son died too and I ask her
when her son died and she says eight years ago
and I say ours was two weeks ago and she doesn't
hear but I think of her as reaching out to me to
join her to be part of this and I said goodbye and
here in Montparnasse I was in a place where
everyone was dead and I was glad of their
company but I thought I don't want to join your
death club, I wished her nothing but the best but
no, I couldn't. Look at you, Samuel Beckett with
your big marble slab.

We went to the same school. We didn't. We could have gone to the same school. It's as if we went to the same school. For chrissake we can't start something because we could have or might have but didn't go to the same school. Or maybe we can. If it feels like home after being away. And yet if it feels so like this, it feels impossible; and if it feels impossible, it's nervy – so forget it, because of course it's not going to happen, too bloody right it won't happen though it could, yes it could.

The school is thirty years old. It's been here for thirty
years so we're going to find out today where your
families were thirty years ago. The hands go up:
My Mum and Dad were in Portugal. My Mum and
Dad were in Nigeria. My Mum was here in Hackney
and my Dad was in Turkey. My Mum was in Portugal
and my Dad was in India. My Mum was in England
and my Dad was in Bangladesh. My Mum and Dad
were in Jamaica. My Mum and Dad were in Antigua.
My Mum and Dad were in the Gambia. And you?

This is Paul.

Where's your family from, Paul?

Congo. Bad man come. Bad man kill my Grandfather.
Bad man come. Bad man kill my Father.

As he says that, I'm remembering a wedding when
my Aunt pointed out her cousin: his parents put him on
a train going east into Russia and he never saw them again.
He turned up on her doorstep in 1946. He never went
back. There was no one left. There's always a there,
so there's always a here. All of us, we've always been

somewhere else. We come out of flats, off fields, away from deserts; off the hills, or away from guns. It's a movement.

We're looking at the photos from the holiday
and Elsie (2) sees a picture of her and me and
says 'Where go mummy gone?' We tell her that
Mummy was just over there, just round the corner
just out of sight . . . she's not happy. I think how
she must see herself as part of her mother . . . or
is it that her mother should be part of her . . . and
perhaps the photo looks to her as if her mother
has left her, not looking after her . . . and then I
think of all those portraits and paintings of
woman by window, woman on couch, man in
mirror, man with dog, woman staring at us,
man with gun, woman bathing, and they're all
on their own, squared off in their oblong frames,
unable to talk to anyone or touch anyone. I suppose
when you look closely at some of them, you can
guess that they might be *thinking* about other
people, and the marks of the life lived are there
on their faces or in the objects in the scene . . .
though somehow the painter so often manages to
make it seem as if all that the person is thinking
about is having their portrait done. At least the
surrealists tried excavating the mind and parading
that all round their portraits; a person ends up

having parts of their world with them in the frame.
With these others, alone and staring, we go on
thinking of ourselves like skittles, removed (is
Elsie saying?) from the mesh that made us and
the mesh we're making.

I think I know why cats eat grass. Something to do with them knowing that all's not well in their guts. So they eat grass, which makes them sick. Then, whatever it was that was making them unwell has gone. It's not inside any more. It's outside. Evacuated. This is not the same as the hairball. Eating their own hair also makes them sick but that's because they lick themselves. The hair just goes in. What I don't know is why cats put the sick where they put it. They bring it to our doorstep. You can tell which sick is from grass-eating and which from hair. The grass-eating sick is a pool of foamy sticky stuff with bits of chewed grass in it. The hairball sick is more solid. Food mixed in and held together by a wadge of hairs. That way you can tell which of the cats has done it. So, some of the hairy sick is ginger. As the sun dries it and the rain washes it, we're left with a skein of ginger hair. Like the twist of wool you find on barbed wire when sheep have pushed through. The mystery, though, is why the cats want to bring us their sick. It feels so like an offering, an act of kindness or generosity. But that doesn't seem likely. When you watch a cat being sick, it looks like they're trying to bring up their whole system. Anything could come out. A kidney maybe. Is it a way of saying they hate us? We sick on you and all that you stand for. Or maybe they think we're Mummy and they just do things like being sick when they're round Mummy. Because deep inside they know that Mummy will clear it up, give them more dinner and lick them all over. Either that or just doing what you do with good friends. You can do anything with good friends. If you were at a football match and you wet yourself, a good friend wouldn't stand up and shout, 'Hey, look, my friend's wet himself.' He would just nod and say, 'Yeah, right. Yeah, I do that sometimes.' Even if he didn't. Bearing that in mind, I just want to say that the cats are OK. They're good to be with. And that sick thing. I didn't mean to draw too much attention to it. I do it myself sometimes.

That was the February when we could see that the reason why was not the reason why. The terrible man had been at his most terrible when they had been helping him. They said he was terrible because he took no notice when the world voted against him. So they took no notice when the world voted against them. This isn't terrible, they said. Then they did terrible things and took his country. This isn't terrible, they said. Waves and waves of us knew this before it happened; we had filled streets and parks and squares all over the world. Our coalition. They rang the newsmen. Ignore it to death, the newsmen said. But we walked on, and we walked on, strangers were friends.

When they do these things, the numbers are un-counted, they flush out, mop up, but no numbers. It was worth it, they say. Believe us, it was worth it. And because they're clever, they always know it was worth it without doing the counting.

He said, I can't stand it any more, it's doing me head in. This place used to be like a village.

– What's the matter with it? I said.

– It's full of foreigners, he said. I love Walthamstow, he said, but I can't stay here. I'm going.

I wondered where but I said nothing. He didn't say anything else, so I said, Where to?

– Spain, he said.

Ah, the unique self. How it strives. How it
competes. How on its own, how individual,
how selfy, it is. What's my self doing today?
It's going about doing things with other selves.
When it gets tired of that, and even as it's doing
that, it seems to be thinking about the things
it has done, or might do, with other selves. My
self is sure that my self is my self and no one
else's. But doubt creeps in: every time my
self thinks about this, it all seems to be thanks
to the band of these other selves that my self
has been doing these things with. My self, then,
seems to have its very own band of other selves
that my self has hung out with, a kind of home
library of other selves. So the thing I call my self
must be no more than how my band of other selves
and my self are getting along? That sounds OK
but there's a problem: there never was a my self
before any other selves were there. There always
were other selves around. Even as I say, 'My self
must be no more than how my band of other selves
and my self are getting along,' I've got it wrong
because the thing that I'm mistakenly calling
'my self' was already doing stuff with other

124

selves. There never was a more selfy self before
it got mixed up with other selves. We are always
others-in-my-selves which would mean that the
sum of us all is really many, many others-in-my-selves.
Let's call us, then, 'our-selves'.

Our-selves don't seem to be random. We aren't like peas boiling in a pot. We clump and gang up. Some gangs impose their our-selves on other our-selves. Let's call these gangs who impose, 'them-selves'. Sometimes our-selves don't like being bossed about and we start to think that we don't have to obey. Sometimes it seems as if the them-selves just do that demanding-to-be-obeyed stuff for the fun of it. Other times it becomes clear that the main reason why they do it is because they want to have their cake and eat it. Sometimes our-selves ask why this should be. Sometimes it seems as if them-selves got the cake by magic, sometimes it might seem that them-selves deserve it as they are so clever, sometimes because they were born with the right to have it. At other times, when things get to a point of great clarity, then thousands, even millions, of our-selves see that the way them-selves get the cake is by not sharing it – which suddenly seems odd because our-selves, who haven't got the cake, remember that our-selves made it. It's this business of them-selves not making the cake and yet keeping it, that means that millions and millions of our-selves are hungry, ill and very, very tired. That would be bad enough, but at various times, them-selves say that the our-selves who made their cake should go to war against the our-selves who made a cake for some other bunch of them-selves. Sadly, this sometimes happens and there is death and injury. And there's grief because no our-selves want to feel our-selves being ripped out. Our-selves aren't always fooled by all this talk of how other our-selves who make other cakes are horrible, inferior and must be competed against, fought against and killed. Our-selves see that we are all no more and no less than our-selves and the best thing to do is get together, make cake and share it.

The worst place to carry a knife is on a plate. All you have to do is tilt the plate as you walk across the room and the knife will fall. Away from the grasp of your hand, it becomes clumsy. You walk across the room and it stabs you in the foot.

A boy stopped me in the street.
– You're fingy, innit, he said.
– I said, Yes.
– He said, I thought so.

I told the primary school my poem:
'Down behind the dustbin
I met a dog called Jim.
He didn't know me
And I didn't know him.'
And a boy at the back shouted,
– How did you know his name was Jim, then?
– And I said, I'm sorry I don't know.
  Are there any more questions?
– A girl said, Who won the FA cup in 1972?
– I don't know that either, I said.
– Do you know what my father's name is? said
  another boy.
– Rumplestiltskin? I said.
– No. It's Patrick, he said.

William Cuffay, born on a ship, homeward bound from St Kitts, in 1788, his grandfather a slave from Africa, his father a slave born on St Kitts. Somehow he came to be brought up in Chatham, his father working as a ship's cook. William became a journeyman tailor. By 1842, he was president of the London Chartists; *The Times* talked of 'the black man and his party'. In April 1848, he spoke at the National Convention in the Literary Insitution, John Street, Fitzroy Square: '. . . things have come to a crisis,' he said, they should not abandon the procession on parliament. On 15 August he was arrested at a meeting in the Orange Tree Tavern, Bloomsbury. According to the spies, he was part of a gang who were going to set London ablaze, with uprisings in Seven Dials, Marylebone, Paddington, Somers Town and Chelsea. It took 103 days to transport him to Tasmania. 'Trade: Tailor; Height: 4/11; Age: 61; Complexion: dark; Head: medium; Hair: black thin; Whiskers: grey; Visage: narrow; Forehead: high; Eyebrows: brown; Eyes: hazel; Nose: broad; Mouth: large; Chin: medium. Rather bald, thin bones and spine deformed. Transported for: Sedition convening a public meeting and speaking at the time. Sentence: Life.' While I was in Australia, I ordered up some records: the three people who came before him on Manuscript Con 14/38 in the Archives Office of Tasmania were John Brown, aged 15, from Middlesex, John Bateman, aged 18, from St Albans and Jonathan Alcock, aged 14, from Lavenham. Mrs Cuffay joined William in 1853 and he was pardoned in February 1857. The *Tasmanian Daily News* tells how he was elected chair of the Meeting held at the Albert Theatre on 24 March 1857. He said that 'he had been attacked by the press but they had to thank the chartists for a new constitution. It contained many of the points of the "People's Charter". They had universal suffrage, they had vote by ballot, equal electoral districts and no property qualifications for members. It was for contending these that he had been sent to this colony. Mr Cuffy then denounced the Master and Servant Act as most atrocious, and that was why he addressed them at the outset as "slaves" and maintained that the makers of that infernal law wanted to reduce the working people to the condition of serfs.' He died in 1870 in Brickfields Invalid Depot at the age of 82. His obituary in the *Hobart Mercury* is headed 'Death of a Celebrity'. It says that 'he was always popular with the working classes' and his 'exertions' along with 'other prominent advocates for the operative classes' led to a satisfactory settlement of the Masters and Servants Act. It says that he 'took a prominent part in election matters, and went in strongly for the individual rights of working men. At a meeting in the Theatre Royal he said, "Fellow-slaves, I'm old, I'm poor, I'm out of work, and I'm in debt, and therefore I have cause to complain." The Superintendent at the Brickfields establishment states that he was a quiet man, and an inveterate reader. His remains were interred in the Trinity burying-ground, and by special desire his grave has been marked, in case friendly sympathizers should hereafter desire to place a memorial stone on the spot.'

He knows we thought he died but he didn't.
Though now he is dying. The doctor's told
him that he is. I'm not happy that the doctor
hasn't said anything to me about it. In this one
tonight, he's unpacking, he's going through
some boxes and bundles. I seem to have packed
up his newspapers and magazines and he's
saying that he doesn't see the point of sorting
them now but I say that I'll help him and we
go through the magazines, saving some,
throwing others. Then, in the dark when I
realize it's been another one of those nights,
I lie awake next to you and your warm skin.

The bus goes on and it's full and it's leaving and it's
laughing and it's going on and it's morning and it's
evening and it's in Punjabi and it's daytime and it's
full and it stops and it's suspicious and it starts and
it's in Ibo and it's shouting and it's shopping and
it's rapping and it's lit up and it's dark and it's shove-up
and it's crying and it's squealing and it's in Dutch and
it's braking and it's in Geordie and it's at the station
and it's skint and it's full of babies and it's full of men
and it's going on and it's past the Vietnamese café and
it's past the tyre depot and it's past the silver car and its
chauffeur and it's waiting for Sinatra to start up and it's
in patois and it's chips and vinegar and it's past the
park and it's full of football and it's a bellyache and it's
full of jokes and it's scared and it's in Arabic and it's
back from school and it's pushing and it's raining and
it's ripe armpits and it's tranks and it's angry and it's
full of yesterday and it's riding under the lights and it's
fucked off and it's the smell of oil and it's pissed and
it's combing and it's kissing and it's packets of rice and
it's cassava and it's over the canal and it's the baby's
bottle and it's over the railway and it's under the cranes
and it's in the shadows of the palaces in glass and it's
in Albanian and it's bleach and it's the homework in

late and it's spuds and it's the *hajib* and it's shoulders next
to backs next to fronts and it's revving and it's too late
and it's too early and it's not enough and it's going on
and it's on time and it's dreaming and it'll get there
today and it'll get there tomorrow